AF413388

TO KNOW YOU

by

E.W. Helmick

Illustrations by

Punky

Way Out West Media Entertainment Group

To all the parents who tirelessly nurture and shape the lives of their children—your faith, love, guidance, and unwavering support are the foundations upon which future leaders, visionaries, and compassionate individuals are built. May this book inspire you to recognize the immense potential within each child and empower you to cultivate the qualities that will help them thrive in the world. Your dedication today is the catalyst for greatness tomorrow.

Eric and Terry Helmick

Contents

Tuck

No man ever steps in the same river twice,

for it's not the same river and he's not the same man.

Heraclitus

You are much like me, and for that I apologize.

You are much like me, and for that, I am endlessly proud.

Hansel is much like you, and for that, I chuckle.

Hansel is much like you, and for that, I am eternally grateful.

Never will I have to worry about you, Tuck. Oh, I do, and I'm forever offering unwanted advice, I know. Forgive me for that. Regardless of the unwanted advice, never do I worry as to whether or not you are going to make it in this life. You are and you will. The reason is simple.

Excuses are not a part of your vocabulary and neither is failure. I've never heard you blame someone else, or exclaim what a failure you have been. I'm ashamed to say, I have said those things, I have blamed others for my shortcomings. This is an important confession, Tuck, because it was you who helped me to see that life can be won, challenges conquered, and success achieved. All one must do is take responsibility for one's life and strive hard each day to make it count. The next day, he must strive harder.

Robert Frost once wrote, "There never was any heart truly great and generous that was not also tender and compassionate." You have always carried inside you a tender and compassionate heart. Though I've seen seasons of angst, and enjoy your skill of cinematic bloodshed, there has always been a deep underlying courtesy towards life. Be it rescuing kittens, baby raccoons, or a young troubled couple, your empathy goes deep and leaves a bountiful impact on life and others.

I see it in the film crews you assemble, the actors and actresses you hire, and the manner to which they respond to you. They have a deep appreciation not only for your level of skill but also for the way you speak to them and treat them. You treat them with kindness and value them with endless courtesy. Where you learned this, I don't know, but it is admirable and stirring to watch. Employers and acquaintances respect you for your cordiality and politeness made evident through patience and humility. A man who approaches life and people in this respect, with a high level of value to which you place upon it and them, is certain to succeed. However, one cannot define success, for, what one man sees as successful pales in comparison to another. I, for one, don't think success is all that important, but rather confirmation that you are doing the right thing at the right season in your life.

When I observe you embracing your beloved wife, teasing her, talking with her, going on small adventures with her, it causes me to reflect on the early days with your mother; filled with penniless days, ice cream, and long conversations on the beach. Much of the time was filled with fear too, apprehension of what we would do next, how we would pay the next bill, how we would ever afford a house of our own, and on and on. Somehow, we did all those things, and somehow, we did it together and with kids, through the seasons of our life.

Pride swells in my heart when I see Hansel embrace you, smile at you, wrestle with you, and laugh with you. When he sees your picture, he says with pride, "Papa!" and I say, "Yes, Hansel, that is your papa, and that is my son, and isn't he first-rate!" Your heart is generous with its care for Star, Hansel, for others, as it has been for your mother and me, and as it will continue to be for as long as you live. In that, Tuck, you have succeeded long before most men accomplish any lackluster prosperity of their own. I believe your motto, Tuck, is that of the great author, F. Scott Fitzgerald when he said, "Never confuse a single defeat with a final defeat."

To know you, Tuck is to be abducted by magnanimity, held hostage by creative lore, drowned in friendship, and given a chance to live each season of life without excuses, without failure.

Estrella

Simplicity is the ultimate sophistication.

Leonardo da Vinci

Da Vinci said it, though I would add that sophistication blossoms from simplicity. Star, how I have grown to love your effervescent innocence! Each day, you approach life with a newness that isn't built on yesterday's "What-ifs" but today's "Why not!"

Life isn't simple; people aren't simple, either. Yet, born from a genuine desire to give life and people the benefit of the doubt, you start each day with the simplest truths: "There is still good in this world, and I can make a difference." Some might call that naivety, others ignorance, but I know better, for I have experienced your simple approach to life and have been blessed by the refreshing innocence to which it is accompanied.

I think sophisticated people learn how to take the best from what a day has to offer. They look for the good aspects of the day, leaving behind the redundant, setting aside the sadness, and plucking from it the genuine moments. Moments that may not be happy and festive, but sophisticated people know how to pick up the pieces of a shattered day and carry them forward into the next, adopting them for good.

As a young mother and wife, it could be said you have not experienced life yet, all the ins and outs, and therefore, you don't have the exposure to be anything but simple. I disagree. You have experiences well beyond many women I know, and you continue to apply the same tenderness to each situation in life. Time and time again, approaching it with a newness and freshness of simplicity.

My mother, Ilah Helmick, was a very sophisticated woman. She dressed to the hilt when going out to dinner with my father and wore diamonds with fashionable docility. You would have loved her, and she you, because though refined, she carried with her through life modesty. Many women in the Bible exemplify modesty and simplicity, but my heart goes out to Ruth, who, though simple, became refined and sophisticated simply by her trust in Naomi. Ruth's story never eludes God in the narrative but is instead seasoned with His heart.

To know you, Estrella is to have my heart seasoned with transparency and poise. To take each day as it comes with the notion it will teach me patience. To anticipate days one by one with innocence and zest. When I lay my head down at night, I will smile and forever remember the Spanish

beauty that introduced me to the delicious picnic basket called Life.

13

Hansel

Nothing shakes the smiling heart.

Santosh Kalwar

There is a very specific day I can point to when God made it clear to me you were a miracle worker. We were walking, you and I, from our two-story home, along the dusty sidewalks of Palisade, Nebraska towards your home after a wonderful warm afternoon at the park. You were at the point of learning to turn your walk into a stride and did so with your elbows pointed back and your head down. Though cracks and uneven rises in the sidewalk were still a challenge to navigate, you did so without hesitation and with great courage. I walked in front of you as you followed in my path, frequently looking back to ensure you were okay. The smell of roses and lilacs mixed with dust was somehow pleasant as it lingered on the nose. Palisade was a quiet village and that afternoon only the sound of your spritely padded steps broke the silence. I turned to see how you were getting along. Without pausing, you looked up, and with pursed lips and broad dimples, smiled at me, with a reassuring, "I'm here, Papa…and I'm keeping up." At that moment something deep inside me, a dark splinter of fear and anxiety, was freed as your luminous smile radiated warmth, confidence, and assurance. At that moment, I knew, Hansel, nothing could shake your good nature, your heart of gold.

Your story began at a very young age. Not just for you, but for your beloved parents. Your gorgeous and charming mother was just eighteen and your genteel father, was twenty-one. Their love for one another was passionate and took precedence over logic and self. Eagerly they courted, and breathlessly they fell in love. They had no money, no place together to call home, and were hopelessly at the mercy of passion. A yearning to be together.

Whenever a child is conceived, there will always be excitement and there will always be fear. Once you have had a child, though it doesn't become easier, it does become a part of one's life for a very long time. The first child, however, is cause for great doubt and anxiety. Doubt that as a parent, you have what it takes to raise a life that will be dependent on you for everything; food, clothing, housing, education, trust, love…everything. And if you're a young parent with little food, clothing, and no housing of your own, doubt and anxiety can dash you upon the rocks and drown you in fear.

I wasn't there the day you were born, but your grandmother Terry was, and got to hold you and whisper tenderly into your tiny ears. I do remember, though, the first day I met you. Grandma Terry had been invited by your Aunt Tasha, Elya, and Tiana to go shopping for Grandma's birthday and have lunch together. They invited your mother to go along and I was to care for you while they were out. We arrived at the home you were staying at near Aunt Tasha and upon entering, found your mother beside herself. She had changed her mind about leaving you behind because, to date, she had not yet left you alone with someone else. With a great deal of coaxing and your mother's tears, the other women finally convinced her to go along and leave you in my care.

First things first; your diaper needed changing. I began the process and the second I pulled off your diaper and turned my back, you peed on everything, including me. After a slight panic attack, I managed to get you clothed again and swaddled in a warm blanket. Then, for the next four hours you and I stared at one another, and I witnessed that eminent smile for the first time. I offered up prayers on your behalf and that of your parents with a hopeful heart. Hopeful that God would bond your heart with Him, but also with your father, Tuck. I knew you would bond with your mother, Star, because I could see the affection she had for you and, furthermore, she was the one providing your food at such a young age. What I desired, was to see an unbreakable bond between you and your father that would tether your hearts together forever. A prayer of that magnitude in a society and day and age when everything a young couple has to go through is steeped in a feeling of chaos was a tall order to be asking for certain.

Do you know what, Hansel? God has answered that prayer time and time again. He has used you to smooth the rough edges marriage often brings with it. You have steadied and brought into focus the dreams your parents desired. Hope has been given a favorable chance because of you. Laughter consumes your home because of your energy and spritely antics. Miracles have overcome your parents and wonder has invaded my heart again and again. The wonder of how much God loves your parents, and your grandparents, to bring someone like you into our lives.

My bad days turned great, and my joys are the results of being in your presence and recalling to mind that warm summer day as we strolled along the dusty streets of Palisade. To know you, Hansel, begins with a smile.

Rise up, my friend, and put your faith in the Lord God Almighty. Trust Him, talk with Him, and step into your place as a mighty man of faith. Honor God with your smile, your kindness, and your love for others. Be courageous in all things throughout your life.

These things have I spoken unto you,
that my joy might remain in you,
and that your joy might be full.

John 15:11 KJV

Alex

Humor is mankind's greatest blessing

Mark Twain

For those capable of understanding you, a world of humor emerges from which their patience will profit!

With a straight face, upon ordinary comment, without any emotional cue, you invite laughter into conversations again and again. Thus, intelligence matters when in the presence of your wit, Alex. You have a talent for sounding serious while eviscerating the subject at hand, but never with unkindness at its core. Humor of this magnitude requires two things: silence and observation. They're more than gimmicks; they are well-crafted tools that allow you to enter a conversation with diplomatic brilliance.

So, over the years, I have tried to prepare myself to be in your presence, to not rely on the general chit-chat of weather and politics, but to dig deeper and see if I might successfully extract a harangue of humor. To do this takes a bit of courage on my part, for I may find myself the brunt of the joke, but it is always worth an attempt to see what you might say. It requires careful study on my part, too, as I watch you observing the conversation, listening for the exact moment you expose the embarrassing, funny, always objectionable truth!

What's even more funny is that your humor has become a conversation among family members. Not to embarrass you or put you on the spot, but countless "gossip" with my children and their siblings and spouses has led to gut-wrenching laughter as we recall your humorous storytelling.

There is a secret to your humor, I know. Something that keeps it kind, moderate, and friendly. It is a private, unpretentious look inward, a self-observation. A simpler definition would be humility. Your jab at society or caprice with a situation or someone is always sprinkled with a dose of meekness. Thus, laughter fills the room because you've simply taken the time to be silent and observe. What a powerful tool you have leveraged, humor, all by being attentive to those in your presence.

We tend to think of the Bible as a staunch telling of religion and the characters who make it up, but I am of the belief that Christ was a fun guy to be around. There are numerous times when, in the presence of His disciples, He responded with humor after careful listening and observation. His humor was dry, His lessons pointed. Alex, you have the hardest job in the world: raise your beautiful children to learn to laugh and to fall in love with Jesus. That can only be done through careful listening and observation of His truth and voice. My prayer for you is that you're able to do just that: hear Jesus' voice and share His love with your children and the world in a tender, humorous manner that molds others into the likeness of Christ.

To know you, Alex is to look into my being and learn to express it without shame.

Tatiana

We were young; you were sweet, I was wild,

with onions in our pockets.

E W Helmick

Ponder I often do, why I cry.

"Don't trust a man who doesn't cry" is my motto.

Because most men don't,

and I want to know why.

Surely my tears have something to do more with joy than sorrow, gladness than misery? Yet in your presence, I find, I cry. Not sobs, not heartache, not lamentation. Then what? What is it that makes me cry when I'm with you?

Commonality is what I think it is. Not commonality as in the populace of the world or hoi polloi we're all the same rank and file and therefore I am moved to tears. Heavens, no! My tears are a shared, tender expression of my adoration for you. You are my weakness, as you are my greatest strength too. The latter is the easiest to identify; a mother who rises day after day, greets her children with anticipation and wonder as she guides day after day. An indefinite and curious ability to live the life of motherhood with pleasure and comity. Each moment spilled into the next with apparent ease and a slight sigh, "Let's do that again," or "You did it!" Never a moment of weakness, never a moment of doubt, always assurance, always, "Well done," added to every accomplishment and "Don't worry," to every blunder. It's an ocean of strength to which you have risen again and again.

You are my weakness, and though I just substantiated your strength in the previous paragraph, we share common ground when it comes to our vulnerability in life. Our powerlessness to change ugly things, fix flawed things, and hold on to frail time. A mountain of Sunday afternoons, gobs and gobs of sunny walks at the zoo, a slather of time…as dusk appears and we face the certainty that our time together is always cut short, there will forever be weakness. Everyone should have someone like you to find their strength and weakness too. It is a humility worth experiencing with another human being, especially one I call my daughter.

To know you, Tiana, is to start the day strong, fully aware that my strength will be courage to those around me. To know you is also to finish my day in weakness. Not regret, not woeful sorrow, but still reflection on the moments that have stolen my heart and left me silent. To know you is to stuff our pockets with onions and invite the world to smell their fragrance and cry a little too.

Oz

Thinking is the talking of the soul with itself.

Plato

There is a photograph of you when you were a little boy, staring out the window on a cloudy afternoon. It is one of the most reflective and veiled pictures I can recall, and one of my favorites. I recollect your mother telling me you were waiting for your father to arrive home from work, which to me, makes the photo even more powerful and tender. Reflective, because, that is what you are doing in the picture, simply reflecting. How I wish I knew everything that was going through your mind. After all, what goes through the mind of a two-year-old? Thus, what makes the picture so wonderful.

For as long as I have known you, Oz, you have maintained a safe place and time for reflection. It's not that your mind has simply wandered off into oblivion and you're lost on some distant planet or dreamy universe. There seems to be a very real place that you like to go in your thoughts, and I believe as Plato so eloquently quotes, *Thinking is the talking of the soul with itself.* What a blissful, wonderful idea, isn't it? To pause, letting everything around you and in you absorb itself with the deepest part of who you are, your soul. Should a man or young man in your case, venture there often, I would think he could alter many aspects of his life. Imagine. Through altercation and confirmation of the mind, the soul is meticulously pierced, until it exits in only its purest form. If one were to learn the art of thinking to the point soul searching wasn't just an allegory, but the truest part of the individual thinking, your life, not to mention the lives of people around you, would be dramatically altered.

It sounds like a good movie, doesn't it? A movie draws you deep into the story and your hope is it gives you something to reflect on, something to believe in or act upon. Thoughts are the same. They can carry you to an imaginary place, but they can also transform the place you are in. Thoughts challenge us, thoughts threaten us, but thoughts that speak to our soul, change us.

As of Monday, November eleventh, Veteran's Day, 2024, the world population was 8,084,667,230. That is a lot of people! Can you imagine how many ideas, thoughts, dreams, and stories are accumulating day after day in the minds of all those individuals? Some old, some young, some strong, some weak – many lonely, and many surrounded by family and friends. Yet, all of their thoughts can transform them and the world they live in. Thoughts become emotions, a seat of affection through which we interact with others. Thoughts become characters through which we develop an appearance and personality. Our psyche, that inner child and inner self develops through what thoughts fill our mind. Finally, thoughts enlist our hearts and our soul, thus making thinking a reasonable pastime. What could be a better use of our time than to engage in an activity that includes your mind, heart, and soul?

Scripture tells us that we are to love God with all our heart, and with all our soul, and with all our mind. Jesus said it was the first and greatest commandment, Matthew 22:37-39. Oz, this should be a thrilling revelation for you, because you have already learned the beauty of reflective and veiled thinking. If you direct those thoughts towards God Almighty, you will be fulfilling the greatest commandment! Then I suspect God will use you in more ways than you can imagine to fulfill the second most important commandment, love your neighbor as yourself. Eight billion people on earth, Oz, and God gave you the gift of contemplation. The delicate ability to pause everything around you as you listen, absorb, and understand. The sixth-century Chinese philosopher, Lao Tzu once said, "Muddy water, let stand, becomes clear." To know you Oz, is to stand in a puddle of muddy water, waiting, watching, as the mind, heart, and soul become clear.

Winry

And though she be but little, she is fierce.

William Shakespeare

If one were addressing a tiger you might say, "My, what a fierce cat!" If the weather was the subject of conversation you may say, "Fierce rain lashed my rooftop!" When I think of you Winry, though you have the spirit of a tiger, I see fierce as a heartfelt and powerful intensity. Well, that's another big word that needs defining, intensity – energy, excitement, fervor. And there you have it, my favorite word, fervor. Intense and passionate feeling.

Winry, I have studied you from afar, and up-close too, and to be in your presence is to be overcome with passionate feelings. Not emotion, but authentic, perfect feelings. A capacity for sensitivity and intuitive under-standing of others and the space around you. Now that's a beautiful thing, my dear young lady! To be able to act and respond to others in a way that gives them courage and excitement about life. It is why I love the word fervor, because it goes against the grain of doing nothing and feeling nothing. Fervor steps out boldly and says, "I've got an appetite for something urgent, a commitment to dedication, an excitement about what's next!" And with animation and vigor, you create space for people to feel invited, and sometimes space for solitude. The key is, you've created something of value for others to experience.

Winry, you are the farthest being from the world of apathy and complacency, and that is why I love being in your presence. Creative people live in that world you know, that place of value and experience. They want to know they are valued and want to experience everything imaginable. So, when I'm with you, I get to experience creativity to the max! I remember many times music playing as with unwavering stability you danced your heart out across the living room floor of your small apartment. Though the apartment was small, when you danced it was as though the walls melted away to an audience of acclaim and the ceiling opened to crystal chandeliers towering high above the stage. All the while with you center stage, dancing. The picture is etched in my mind forever. Music is in your heart, and many times you would just sit and sing a favorite melody, or a made-up one. I couldn't always understand what it was you were singing, but I shan't ever forget the gentle voice behind the song.

On one occasion, before you were talking sentences I could understand, Grandma Terry and I brought our friends Steve and Donna Denning over to meet you and your siblings. We had a wonderful time together, ate some lunch, and watched you dance. At one point, Steve had to use the restroom, and your mother, Tiana, directed him to the master bathroom. He went to use the restroom, and you decided to follow. Later, he told me what had taken place. It seems he went and used the bathroom, and when he came out, you were outside the door to greet him. Looking up into his bearded face, you chattered and chattered. He stooped over and looked at you and said, "Winry, although I don't know what you just said, I'll cherish this moment for the rest of my life." And he has.

To know you, Winry, is to be overcome by your ferocious appetite for life, while melodic themes melt away the walls of time, the ceiling is lifted off heavy hearts, and we dance to shadows of acclaiming audiences shouting, "She is little, she is fierce, she is fervor!" And with those words in my heart tonight, I lay myself to sleep happy and filled with feelings. And tomorrow, I'll wake up with an appetite for life, thanks to you my small, fierce Winry!

Nausicaa

There is a famous photo of your mother with Uncle Hunter, Aunt Tasha, and Elya, taken in Santa Barbara, California the day we were headed to a western event and barbecue. Everyone is dressed up, including your mother, with a cowboy hat and wool vest. It's quite a festive picture, but what is etched on my mind forever is the wonderful, sassy expression on your mother's pursed lips. It's as though she were saying, "I'm cheeky, I'm charming, filled with dash! C'mon, let's dance and give life a zing!" And so, she has, and continues to with you by her side. Well, hardly by her side…perhaps now it is with your mother in tow! Man was made in the image of God, and you Nausicaa, are the image of your mother.

The first dozen times I held you in my arms, it was easy and euphoric, your eyes glued to mine, my heart melted to yours. As you grew older, however, and due to the distance missions and travel brought your grandmother, Terry, and I, your feelings of trust broke down, and visit upon visit I found you weren't quite so eager any longer to climb up in my lap or let me hold you. It's a spell all children go through, wanting a mother more than any other. It's a good spell, one filled with the enchantment only a mother can create from a tender place of understanding.

Sitting in your home during Grandma's and my visits, you would watch me from a distance as though you remembered our former bond. You seemed eager to try again and would venture just close enough for me to reach out and hug you, but then with a whisper of little feet, back to Mother, you pattered. Nausicaa, I think God sees us like that sometimes. He's so eager to have us in His arms, and He waits so patiently until we come close enough for Him to reach out and lift us up into His warm embrace and sweet bearded cheek. I don't know if God has a beard, but if He does, it's fun to imagine what it might be like, isn't it?

Eventually, over time, I earned your trust, and again we found ourselves glued to one another in a fond manner of speaking. When I pick you up and look into your eyes, smell your silky blond hair, and listen to your giggle, it is as though I am transported back in time, holding your mother when she was a little girl, just like you, filled with so much liveliness, so much delight, so much curiosity about life.

Being like someone can be glorious Nausicaa. Because you are a mirror of not only beauty but memories. When people look at you, they see into the past and can remember good and sweet days, as well as sad and tearful days. That's not a bad thing to reflect on life, it's a good way of remembering all we can be thankful for. That is what you do for me, Nausicaa, you help me to find thankfulness deep within my heart. I'm thankful for your grandmother Terry. I'm thankful we had so many wonderful children. I'm thankful all my children, your aunts and uncles, love Jesus with all their hearts. I'm thankful for your mother. Your beautiful mother. Her smile, her laughter, all reflected in you. I'm thankful for you too, Nausicaa, and for the love you bring to this world through kaleidoscope eyes. Do you know what a kaleidoscope is? A kaleidoscope is just a sophisticated way of seeing light. It's very simple, yet extraordinarily beautiful. You are my kaleidoscope, Nausicaa, and when I'm with you, I see a complex world made simple and extraordinarily beautiful. To know you, Nausicaa, is to shout out loud, "I'm cheeky, I'm charming, filled with dash! C'mon, let's dance and give life a zing!"

Kanna

My favorite stories are the ones your eyes tell

John Mark Green

Curiosity runs through my mind as I watch you stare at me. You've bent your neck to such a degree, I can't help but think how painful that must be. But then again, perhaps not, since you are only six months old and I've seen babies contort into all sorts of odd shapes. I'm intrigued at how long you can stare at me unblinking, and I at you. It's easy for me to explain the fascination; you're beautiful, fearfully so, and wonderfully made, scripture says so, Psalm 139:14. Yet there's so much more to it that demands definition. Watching you watching me, I sense that already our souls are somehow matched, paired together like a spider's web that is nearly invisible until the morning dew settles upon its fragile threads. Watching you watching me, I feel exposed, like you somehow know me better than I know myself, or perhaps you are experiencing innocence, something I only long to remember.

Watching you watching me, I'm certain you're looking for a reason to trust me, and I, a reason to be trusted. You can trust me, I assure you, but my life at sixty-three is much different than yours of six months. Trusting others is all you have to count on, whereas I've spent my life learning to trust others and have them trust me in return.

A smile breaks across your tiny lips and you blink, though it looks more to me like you fluttered your eyelids at me. The hardness inside me is moved, yet I remain motionless, still, returning the smile, which grows into a wide grin, so wide it hurts my cheeks. What else can I do? I am in the presence of a child who thinks I'm worth spending time with, someone who thinks I hung the moon. I would if I could, Kanna. The only thing limiting me is me, I suppose, but here in your presence, just the two of us, I suspect anything is possible and anything is obtainable. If only you were to ask, I would do anything for you.

We don't just stare at one another. A few precious moments of staring and we both give in to a big hug and a kiss. Holding you in my arms is like holding a stick of butter. You're so tiny, you simply melt in my arms as I pull you close, smell your hair, and whisper how much I love you in your ear. You'll let me hold you forever, and if time wasn't ticking away, I would. Thus, to know you, Kanna, is to waltz with you in my arms forever, buried in the knowledge that someone trusts me enough, finds my love innocent enough, to hold them, our souls in harmony, one with another. Know that I pray for you daily, in hopes you will give your life to the Lord Jesus at a young age, and you will find yourself smiling at Him, as He is already smiling at you.

Hunter

Legacies are footprints of legends
who walked among men

Michael Bassey Johnson

"And for a moment, we were mighty men."

These are the words that echo in my mind over and over again as I reflect upon our swim across Australia. You, Tuck, and I, mighty men, men with a cause, men with the courage to step out and defy the odds stacked against us, the naysayers, even our skeptical minds. Though I'll forever feel I failed the attempt and dispirited the team, you championed not only me, but also the team, and everyone we met along the way.

How could you swim all day, then entertain and encourage others with words of kindness, physical chores, and duties, and find time to record a personal video journal besides? Mighty is the only word that describes your effort then and your efforts now, Hunter. An indomitable existence that carries with it the idea that anything is possible at any time, all the time. I know you have doubts and fears, who doesn't, but you somehow dissolve disbelief into certainty and intimidation into an ordinary existence of belief. I know, without a doubt, Jesus has that effect on you, and I know you attribute any confidence or strength to Him. That in itself is a legacy, I think; to attribute your courage and strength to Christ. I've always said, however, that courage and strength, though gifts of the Creator, are most often required, to be mustered up on our own. Agree or disagree, I believe the mighty men of David, mustered their strength, and it was God who then further sanctioned their cause.

Time and time again I have seen you muster your courage and strength. I think the most obvious example is when you told me the story of Cydney, lying in the hospital in Kosovo after losing the baby, and you were not allowed to be with her. You sat in the car and screamed at the devil, the deceiver, the robber of life. Like Shackleton, hobbled and entombed in an icy landscape, you sat in your car alone, fully aware of the loss you had experienced as a couple, conscious of the temptation to blame the creator, and yet willing to give Him your weakness and let Him turn it to honor. Grief unsurmountable turned to peace, courage summoned, and strength reunited with hope.

When a toxic breakdown and disagreement between two of our team members seemed as though it was going to burst into a fury of insults and hurt, you stepped in and listened to each young man, offering them not just resolve, but courage to stay the course and focus their attention on bettering themselves. Peace won, and the team moved forward with newfound strength.

Mighty men, as we read in scripture, moved in such a fashion that their exploits though incredible, stemmed from a belief system that they had the right to execute judgment and firmness over their enemy and any situation that required tenacity. From the sinew of their being, they were made for this cause; authority, energy, jurisdiction, and command. These words all mean the same thing in general, but each is very specific too.

Command is your stance in the face of fear and doubt. Jurisdiction is the flag of victory, which you wave in the enemy's face. Your energy, like an ocean wave, moves forward with force and influence. Your authority, deep seated in the knowledge that you can do all things in Christ. Thus, Hunter, to know you is to step out onto the ice with unwavering courage, to shout at the devil in victory, and give honor to the King of Kings. To know you is to walk among mighty men.

Cydney

Whatever beauty we behold, the more it is distant, serene, and cold,

the purer and more durable it is. For it is better to warm ourselves

with ice than with fire.

Henry David Thoreau

The moment I laid eyes on you, I thought, "What beauty has entered my being?" I remember a feeling of breathlessness and wonder. There is a whisper of truth to Thoreau's definition of beauty in your presence: distant, serene, and cold. The anatomy of each characteristic begs to be appreciated.

I have never thought of you as distant but like the setting sun, mesmerizing in your ability to capture my imagination. Alfred Lord Tennyson defined you best: "Knowledge comes, but wisdom lingers, and I linger on the shore." How I would love to visit this distant shore with you! With all its sunsets, tides of change, and dreams that put the viewer into a trance, a distant journey.

Serene is the word I think best describes you, Cydney. Composed, smooth, peaceful, cool. Few things other than myself cause you anxiety, and fear is irrelevant in your daily walk with Christ. In your presence, people experience the beauty that is filled with peace. Ancient philosophers had simple, objective definitions of beauty and peace. Beauty is the splendor of order. Peace is the rest of the order. Perhaps more simply, beauty is harmony and peace, the listening ear. The Bach Prélude et Fugue en Ré Majeur is a classical contrapuntal, polyphonic piece in which two or more voices are introduced at the beginning in imitation. I watched an organist play this piece and was mesmerized by her ability to introduce the piece with her right hand, echo the theme with her left hand, and eventually echo the theme with her feet, too. Thus, your serene presence continues to echo a deep, mesmerizing theme of life.

For it is better to warm ourselves with ice than with fire. I love the scene in David Mamet's film *The Edge*, where Anthony Hopkins is explaining to Alec Baldwin how to make fire from ice. Baldwin is anxious and deeply distraught by the fact they are trapped in the wilderness with no hope of rescue and little hope of survival. Hopkins, on the other hand, is positive as he turns the ill-fated journey from desperation to hope, explaining that one can make fire from ice. Thoreau tells us that beauty is made purest if it is born of the distant, serene, and cold. My thoughts on how your beauty is both distant and serene have been outlined. Cold, however, is as unique as a one-of-a-kind snowflake. Your beauty is better defined if I were to use "glory" instead of cold. Paul writes of his glory in II Corinthians 11:30, "If I must needs glory, I will glory of the things which concern mine infirmities." Paul gives an account of his suffering, not out of vain glory but out of honor to God. As others boast of their strength and success, you, Cydney, bring brisk authenticity to life. To know you, Cydney is to listen to the complexity of the world while being refined by its splendor as the briskness of life refreshes our hearts and minds.

Adelaide

Sometimes the smallest things

take up the most room in your heart.

Winnie the Pooh

Promise and Kiah. Names now spoken in a whisper with adoration. They were not part of your life, Adelaide, nor mine, but they will be part of our future and eternity. The night I learned that your mother had lost Pristina while pregnant, we were in the village of Pango on the island of Efate in Vanuatu in the South Pacific. Grandma Terry and I felt so far away and so lost because we could not be with your mother and father to help them or console them. At midnight, unable to sleep, I walked out onto the beach and stared up at the stars. Millions upon millions of stars, the Milky Way, and even a far-off galaxy, all staring back at me, reminded me of how small we really are, and how big God is. Tears ran down my cheeks as I prayed for your parents and begged Him for a miracle.

Miracles, I have found are far and few between. It might be that they are just sometimes harder to see than at other times. Perhaps if we paused long enough, we would see an abundance of miracles in our lives and those of others around us. Looking for miracles I suppose, gives us hope, and as your great-uncle, Jim, always said, "Hope must be the objective." And so it was that, on April 30th, 2021 you were born, Adelaide Zoe Helmick to Mister and Missus Hunter and Cydney Helmick. You, Adelaide, gave all of us hope that from a lonely beach in the South Pacific, around the world, to the far reaches of Kosovo, our prayers were answered by a loving, big God.

"Big God" is a phrase I think you're familiar with. How do I know? Because I've heard your prayers, and watched as by faith, you held coins to the wall and asked God to make them stick. What a crazy idea! Sticking coins on the wall and asking God to make them stick! You know what? I think God has a bit of silliness and craziness in Him, enough to do anything you ask and believe of Him. He's a big God, isn't He? The idea of asking Him to stick coins to the wall, heal a sick person, or give us joy when we are sad is our way of saying, "Father, I believe in you so much that just sitting here waiting on you is enough, but if you would show up and lift my spirits, heal a sick person, or adhere a coin to the wall, my faith would grow, and you would be exalted." So it is with you, Adelaide, your heart planted in a furrow of God's warmth and love for His glory.

You can tell a lot about a person if you just sit and spend time with them. You may not remember our visit when we came to Oregon in the summer of 2023, but I remember it like it was yesterday. It was the first time Grandma Terry and I got to meet you in person. We had talked on the phone and seen your face on the computer, but now we got to know you in person! What a wonderment you were. The amount of knowledge you possessed about so many things, your love for every kind of food and taste, and the respect you showed your parents. It's not peculiar for a two-year-old to love their parents, but you somehow have a deeper respect and understanding of the sadness they had experienced, now turned to utter joy with you, their beautiful daughter.

Adelaide, my heart swells each time I see a picture of you, hear your voice, or lift you up in prayer. I somehow feel safe in your presence as though you know the secret of gladness. It is as though you understand the deepness of God's love and that somehow gives you the energy, courage, and poise to navigate life. Life for a two-year-old isn't too difficult I should think, but you give life to those around you in a way that is fruitful and credible. To know you, Adelaide, is to hold a coin in my fingertips, place it on the wall, and believe that God will adhere it, if for nothing else, His good pleasure, and our innocent faith. Bless you for helping me to believe more deeply. I'll tell you a little secret. I still haven't got a coin to stick on the wall. Not for the lack of trying, and sometimes they stick for just a short while before falling to the ground. Each time they fall, my heart falls too, but all I have to do is remember the sounds of your sweet voice, your treasured giggle, and my heart is lifted and I try again. Thanks for living!

Miles

A man need only look behind him to see his strength

in the gentle footprints he leaves behind in the sand.

E W Helmick

Can you imagine what it would be like to have the power to give people happiness? In a world of unhappiness, it would be quite the superpower, wouldn't it? When you were born, Miles, you were a big guy. Ten pounds at birth is what I'm told! Grandma Terry and I were with your mother and father just before you were born. We were visiting them in Oregon and stayed with your grandparents, Becky and Kevin, who were in the middle of remodeling their kitchen. So, meals were cooked out of a little kitchen closet and served on the back patio or in the sitting room. Your mother was very ready to give birth and spent the days resting and eating and watching your sister, Adelaide, entertain Grandma Terry and me in her very small plastic house in her bedroom. We visited the birth center where you were to be born and the midwives were pleased with your mother's health and simply said, "Just a little while longer." Well, the time came and we had to go back to our own homes and responsibilities.

A month later, you were born. Ten pounds born! I don't mean to keep hammering how big you were at birth, but my friend, there is strength in big things! Why is that important? Because, Miles, you were born into a world where people are sometimes filled with fear. A time of war. When men lack courage. Not all men of course, but it only takes one man to shout "fire" to bring an army of firetrucks to his cause. My favorite character in the Bible was Samson. I think he must have been a big guy when he was born too. The Bible says that when he was born, *the child grew, and God blessed him,* Judges 13:24. That word *grew*, means to become *large* as in body, mind, and honor. Samson was a tower of nourishment and excellence! I think, Miles, you too were born a tower of nourishment and excellence! When I say nourishment, what I mean is sustenance – what you're made of, and by that, I mean deep, deep inside your heart and soul…what are you made of? That's a fun question to think about, isn't it? What are you made of deep inside? The Bible says we're all made in God's image, but there is something more that makes you who you are, Miles, and that comes from your mother and father. Invisible pieces of your parents are now a part of you and they make up not only your genetics, eyes, and hair, they create in you something excellent, just like Samson's parents gave him something spectacular, too.

What is that invisible ingredient inside you, Miles? It's simple really. It's one of the simplest ingredients a mother and father can add to their children's lives. It's Jesus. You might ask yourself; how can Jesus be a part of me, I'm very young still, and though very big…I'm simple and haven't even learned to talk or walk yet. That's the beauty of this ingredient, Jesus. It can be inside you without you realizing it for a very long time, and then one day, you have the chance to ask yourself, "What makes me me?" There it rises to the surface, Jesus.

Now, like lots of ingredients in bread and cookies and savory meats, the spices aren't always that easy to discern. You have to taste the food and work hard to figure out what you're tasting. Jesus isn't quite so hard to discern, but you will have to come to the point at which he is a secret ingredient in your life that you will want to always have with you.

So, what do Jesus, recipes, strength, and Samson all have to do with you Miles? It's very simple really. The day you were born, God poured out His favor on a family that loves having Jesus be the ingredient of everything they do. And because of you, as author George Bernard Shaw pointed out, "A happy family is but an earlier heaven." In other words, Miles, to know you is to have a glimpse of the blissful experience that awaits us one day in heaven, alongside a strong, powerful, loving God.

Troy

You cannot do a kindness too soon

because you never know how soon it will be too late.

Ralph Waldo Emerson

I've never met a more sincere and generous man than my father, Richard R. Helmick, that is, until I met you, Troy.

Generosity, in its truest sense, costs you nothing. There is never a second thought, doubt, or fear of not having enough. At its core, it is unselfish and voluntary every time. Winston Churchill nailed it when he said, "We make a living by what we get, but we make a life by what we give." Thus, you have given life to many people around you, some weak, others desperate, some in need of encouragement, all beneficiaries of your generosity.

The only person who remembers a generous act is the one on the receiving end. I can recall many times you have blessed Terry and me, sometimes when we were desperate for help, other times when your heart was moved by circumstance. The person giving, however, rarely has an accounting of his bounteousness. It would be absurd, really, to have a black book filled with all the giving a person had given, filled with names and facts of all the situations in which others required rescue. It is much like our Savior, Troy, giving bountifully without regret, without report, without the need for explanation, just a free gift to receive.

I have said many times to Terry, "Troy has the heart of Jesus." A heart that is not only generous but genuine. You can muster up all the reasons why you are the way you are, but Winnie the Pooh said it best, "Doing nothing often leads to the very best something." It's the idea of mindfulness, the practice of being present at the moment and fully engaged with your surroundings. That is such a clear picture of you, Troy! Completely engaged with your surroundings, even when you're just sitting on a boat, the shore, or your driveway, and everyone in your presence is equally engaged because of you. This is the mindset of Jesus, completely engaged with not only His surroundings but also those He was encompassed with.

Troy, I pray for you every day. Every day! My prayer is that Jesus encompasses you completely with the same generosity and kindness you have shown others so that you come to realize the fastidious characteristics that define you are derived from Him. To know you, Troy, is to be drawn into the supernatural presence of God as I experience His love for me through your simple acts of kindness. Know Him, trust Him, call upon His name, and become acquainted with the most generous of all.

63

Natasha

Nobody but a Princess could be so delicate.

Hans Christian Anderson

Delicate is not the first word most people would use to describe you, but then again, most people don't know you. The lion's share of people who do know you, I suppose have not invested the time required to experience you. Ah, so it is…to truly know someone requires time. A moment of pause, a duration of attention, a slowness of pace. Still, delicate may not be the first thing people see when they ease their own tempo of life and experience yours, but it's a start.

It isn't because you are difficult to understand. It is because you are forever pouring yourself into others' lives, making them valuable far beyond self. Thus, for someone to experience you, they must keep up the tempo of a life filled with infatuation, enthusiasm, and avocadoes. I mention avocadoes because I know your affection for them, but also because as someone once said, "Spread love as thick as you would an avocado!" In your presence people are smothered in affection and goodwill. It is your way, it is how you receive others and interact with the world, reckless as it is deliberate. Reckless in that you abandon reason for kindness and deliberate in your disregard for self.

Thus far, I've chosen to define *delicate* with contentious alternate words, but therein lies the secret of your delicateness. It is surrounded by a world of aggression, a society of acrimony, and people of apathy. While everything around you is determined to crush what is weak, you continue to rise to what is fragile. People.

The problem really is people, isn't it? You've said so yourself, how people make such a mess out of their own lives. They litter their feelings for others to tramp on, and hang lazy thoughts out on the line for the dross of society to expunge. If we treated people how they treat one another, how they treat us, surely, we would be justified.

I've seen it many times, the outpouring of self to see others rise to greatness. Our fire department experience together had many such occasions. You were the smallest person in the department, certainly not the strongest when it came to brawniness, but repeatedly, it was you who was at the forefront of every extraction, fire, and icy water training exercise shouting to the others, "C'mon, this is going to be fun!" So, the rest of us fell in line and followed you into the smoke, only your voice and the reassurance we were going the right way to guide us. Life is full of smoke and people need someone like you to encourage them to keep going, to find their way out of the smoke and into the freshness of life and that breath of fresh air.

Over and over, Tasha, you have encouraged me to prepare myself physically and mentally, to put on that heavy gear of life, oxygen tanks, gloves, boots, mask, and step forward into the smoke and searing flames. When I am most afraid, it is your voice in the midst that says, "You've got this papa, c'mon, this way!" And, voilà, each time, I exit unharmed, remove my mask, take in a deep breath and say, "I did it!"

All men were created equal, then a few became firefighters including a small, delicate young lady at the age of eighteen, named Natasha.

People. Are they ordinary, callous, and ugly? Or worthy, elegant, and delicate? Anyone who takes time to be in your presence will know the answer, for to know you, Tasha, is to spread love as thick as you would a delicate, delicious avocado.

Jonathan

He who loves the coming of the Lord is not he who af-

firms that it is far off, nor is it he who says it is near, but

rather he who, whether it be far off or near, awaits it

with sincere faith, steadfast hope, and fervent love.

Saint Augustine

Upon our first introduction, I was deeply moved to hear the story of your mother's passing. It brought to mind a similar story that took place when I was in Junior High. A friend had been on vacation with his family when an accident occurred on their return home. Several immediate family members were killed, including his mother. After a few weeks of healing physically, he returned to school with bandages, a broken leg, and crutches. While waiting in line to enter the classroom, a fellow student nonchalantly asked, "What happened to you!" My friend replied with a gentle, "I was in a car accident." "Wow, crazy! What happened? Was anybody else hurt?" the student exclaimed dramatically. "My mother," said my friend. "What happened?" asked the student, a thrill in his voice. My friend looked up at me, tears streaming down his face. In a whispered, barely audible voice, he said, "She died." Never will I forget the pain I felt in my heart, the shame I felt for my fellow student, and never will I forget the tears streaming down my friend's face. I have often wondered what happened to him, how he navigated life without his mother, whether he was able to overcome the situation, and most of all, whether he is now steadfast in his character as a man and whether he knows the Lord.

Steadfast is a characteristic easily attributed to the scriptures but less often attributed to how a person navigates life. Yet, steadfast is how I have always experienced you, Jonathan. From the very first time we met and through the years, you remain steadfast. Steadfast begs a definition: unwavering, firm in purpose, resolution, and faith. You could build a kingdom on such noble principles! Instead, you have built a family. Someone once said, "What can you do to promote world peace? Go home and love your family." What a blessing it has been for me to watch you mature into the man you are today. From preaching to beekeeping, building to farming, watching you raise your family has been a delightful pastime.

I've said being a father is the hardest job in the world. Mothers, perhaps, would disagree but, nonetheless, understand my argument. At a young age, a fierce wind claimed the life of your mother, yet you somehow resolved to turn head-on into that wind and prevail. "To him that knoweth not the port to which he is bound, no wind can be favorable." But you somehow knew the direction you must turn in, and with singleness of purpose, kept your eye on the goal. In turn, you have brought your family not into the safety of port, but instead, remain a valiant ship upon the high seas, facing the gales with steadfastness and faith.

To know you, Jonathan, is to hear the intimate calling of a disciple who proclaims, "This one thing I do, forgetting those things which are behind, and reaching forth unto those things which are before, I press toward the mark for the prize of the high calling of God in Christ Jesus!" Philippians 3:13-14

Amanda

There's no such thing as perfection,

but in striving for perfection, we can achieve excellence.

Vince Lombardi

The endeavor for perfection will always come across as arrogant, heartless, authoritative, and unfortunately, heartless. Only those who function in that place can understand. "Be a yardstick of quality. Some people aren't used to an environment where excellence is expected." Steve Jobs. Not that I expect people to be perfect, but I do think we should all be striving for excellence. Amanda, this is what I love about you! Your drive for excellence is bold and deliberate, and what the Psalmist had in mind when he wrote, "But to the saints that are in the earth, and to the excellent, in whom is all my delight." Psalm 16:3 The word excellent is noble, principled, and worthy. Why, for heaven's sake, that incites fear in others, I don't know, and I know you, like me, have experienced repercussions of such thinking. Regardless, it is what I love about you!

Daniel had an extraordinary spirit, knowledge, and insight, was able to explain enigmas, and was able to solve difficult problems. If you walk in what is true, honorable, right, pure, lovely, of good repute, excellence, and things worthy of praise, you're going to be walking a path that leads to perfection. Undoubtedly, you will never be perfect, nor will I, but we shouldn't be a threat either. Thus, here is where the striving for perfection, a life of excellence, turns to something else, something much deeper and meaningful. Amour, amour, véritable! Love, genuine love.

The outpouring of love you have for others is unmatched among most people I know who proclaim Christ as their savior. Of course, my beautiful wife, Terry, fits the profile, but what else can she do in the presence of my perfection?! Seriously, Amanda, I have seen you set aside your drive for excellence and replace it with nurturing love time and time again. The most obvious, of course, is the affection you have for your husband and children, but I have been privileged to see it expressed in a much deeper, mysterious way.

Upon our first encounter, you met our uncertain mood and circumstances with a beautiful smile, delightful hospitality, and an outpouring of love. There wasn't a moment when I felt threatened, uncertain, or questioned what might happen next. When you're in the presence of excellence and love, it is, as William Shakespeare described, a "winged cupid painted blind." What a lesson the world could learn from you, Amanda, if they were to simply blind themselves to what they thought were their rights, deafen ears to lies, and step out with perfect love for one another. "Perfect love casts out fears," I John 4:18, and so we come back full circle to the introductory theme of perfection. It isn't such a bad idea to strive for perfection, to achieve excellence, for to know you, Amanda, is to achieve a most excellent love so that I might be worthy of the Father's delight.

HONEY COMB

Abby

Someday, when the pages of my life end,

I know that you will be one of the most beautiful chapters.

Author Unknown

Bitterness has turned sweet as a honeycomb. Sorrow has ripened into gladness. The King's heart has shed a thousand tears, but at the break of every new day, he gives thanks for you, my dearest Abby.

You are the visual, accomplished, foolproof work of the King. From the moment you were conceived to the moment where you now sit and read these words. The King has shown His favor over you and the angels sing His praise, *For as the rain cometh down, and the snow from heaven, and returneth not thither, but watereth the earth, and maketh it bring forth and bud, that it may give seed to the sower, and bread to the eater: So shallmy wordbe that goeth forth out of my mouth: it shall not return unto me void, but it shall do that which I please, and it shall accomplish that for which I send it.* Isaiah 55:10-11

Imagine with me for a moment, a King, the God of heaven and earth, pleased with what He spoke and what He accomplished in you, Abby. Never an error, never a regret, never abandoned. That is what the word "void," means; empty and ineffectual. Do you know what the opposite of the word void is? Worthy. You are worthy, Abby, as God's mouth has spoken. Now, what will you do with that worth? It's like having an account in a bank that someone has given to you and said, "This is your account, all the money and all the treasures inside that vault, do with it as you wish." My mind spins at all the wonderful things you and I could do with a vault full of money! But what do we do, when everything that is of value isn't inside a locked vault, but inside our heart?

The King's Heart was written for you and your birth mother, Natasha, knowing full well that you would have two mothers! It is quite the allegory as kings and queens, princesses and evil spirits vie for the attention of one beautiful young maiden. An allegory turned true; a fairytale become verity. It is a very real and spiritual story with people who have touched earth and heaven symmetrically. The characters shed tears, wrestle fears, laugh with joy, and must forever rise to the best of who they are, with hearts of conviction.

So, I ask again, what will you do with your worth? Watching you grow I see a young lady filled with life, a girl who brings great joy to everyone she encounters, and those who are closest to her. A maiden who remembers her humble beginnings yet thrives on a future of blessing and prosperity. This is what I experience on the outside from a distance, Abby. You and I both know that what counts is what is on the inside, and what is planted deep within your heart. How much God loves you and how much you love him in return.

Adoption is such a fantastic miracle. And you, like me, have gotten to experience it not once, but twice. For once we were adopted into our parents' home and once, we were adopted into the Kingdom of Christ. How excellent and how wonderful that we share binary adoption! Someone once asked me, "Do you wonder who your real parents were?" I didn't give it another thought when I answered, "Of course not. I live with my real parents!" I had wonderful parents, who loved me and cared for me in amazing ways, far beyond what my biological parents were able to do. You, however, know of your biological mother, Natasha, and in fact, have an intimate relationship with her and love her dearly. And because of your alacrity to know her, and believe in her, you have the sweetest answer within your heart, "I know my mother, both of them." To know you, Abby, is to be loved by you unconditionally, to have all wrongs made right, flaws turned into blessings, and tears to joy. The King's heart, once only a cold green emerald stone, now blisters with radiant warmth, made whole by the one true King who shall do what he pleases and accomplish all that is worthy. You, Abby, are worthy in the King's eyes and in the hearts of those who know you best.

Caleb

I would maintain that thanks are the highest form of thought,

and that gratitude is happiness doubled by wonder

G. K. Chesterton

I will never forget the day I first held you in my arms. I had been at work all day and news of your birth came by phone. Apprehension filled my heart. Can you imagine, a grown man being nervous or anxious about meeting a baby for the first time? Still, as I made my way up to the room where Natasha had given birth to you, I wondered, what would I say, what should I say? Were there any words that could express how I was feeling, or how she might be feeling?

The room was filled with activity; a nurse was talking with Natasha, your grandmother, Terry, was holding you, and your mother, Amanda, was talking with someone on the phone, I suspect your father. Grandmother Terry approached me and placed you in my arms before I could object. It wasn't but a split second before tears filled my eyes as I looked down at you and whispered the words, "Thank you, Lord." Thanks, the highest form of thought, and the sudden gratitude of happiness doubled by wonder.

Of course, there was happiness, everyone was grateful for a safe birth for you and delivery for Natasha, who radiated from her bed, eagerly watching me as I held you in my arms, the apprehension of moments before, withered away. Then, something else set in, and it's only now I realize what it was that I was beginning to feel. Wonder. A double portion, to be sure. Not a wonder that leaves one perplexed or in doubt; this was a wonder filled with marvel, curiosity, astonishment, and just a little uncertainty.

Life is a marvel all in itself, but life in the form of a baby is mysterious and awe-inspiring. It brings with it astonishment that life is possible in such a small being, and leaves you with a deep curiosity as to who this person will become, what will they be like, how will they know me, will they like me, what will they look like when they grow older. On and on the mix of emotions went for as long as you were in my arms.

Then, uncertainty. It is fair to say it was worry. Worry over Natasha, and worry over you and your mother and father. How, in all its complexity of birth, life, and lives touched, will this young baby, react to his adoption, to both his mothers, and to me and Terry, his grandparents?

The aforementioned question is no longer a question, nor has it left any uncertainty in my life. Your life hence has been seasoned with gratitude and happiness, with Jesus at its core. Only one thing remains on my mind now, and that is how your gratitude will turn to happiness for you and those closest to you. The answer is simple. For to know you, Caleb, is to walk in this life with happiness, with a double portion of wonder for the mysteries of God.

Gil

My hair is troublesome and curly,

my heart, agreeable and sweet

E W Helmick

A hair full of troublesome curls, a heart that is friendly and sweet, that is how I have experienced you, Gil, the few times I have been privileged to be in your company. In a world that has become most troublesome, people need someone who carries some degree of enthusiasm for curls and agreeability!

I too had curly hair when I was your age and I didn't like it very much. It was difficult to manage when it grew out and wasn't in style if I cut it short. I had a terrible time feeling good about myself and wanted just plain old straight hair like everyone else. Funny, isn't it? Now my hair is short, and I don't worry much about curls, but I do adore them. If given the chance, I find myself burying my face in my granddaughter's curly hair, taking a long sniff, and could fall asleep in that pile of curls!

Curly hair attracts attention, and it's kind of your signature for now. It's like saying, "Hey, what you see on my head is who I am inside; fun, like a corkscrew!" People can't ignore someone with that kind of energy and attitude about life!

There's something else, too, that attracts people to you, and that is the miracle story of your existence. You were born to wonderful parents, who desired deeply the chance to have a child of their own. Voilà! Here you are! A miracle! Not just because you are made in God's image, but because He's given you unique features that your siblings don't have. You have an imprint of your mother and father in the curly hair that you wear and the sweet, agreeable heart that is much like your father's. These are important possessions to remember as you grow older, because one day your hair may straighten, and you'll find your heart struggles to be sweet and agreeable as a disagreeable world closes in. Remember this, Gil…as Dr. Suess once wrote, "Today you are you! That is truer than true! There is no one alive that is you-er than you!"

To know you, Gil, is to taste one's own identity the way God intended us to; agreeable, sweet, curly, you-er than you!

Dustin

Keep looking up…that's the secret of life.

Charlie Brown

I have never met someone whose outlook on life is more positive than yours, Dustin. Regardless of the circumstances or obstacles set before you, confident and absolute is your approach to each situation. It is a quality I admire, yet I have been unable to apply it to my own life with any great success. Clint Eastwood said once, "If you think it's going to rain, it'll rain." Thus, I've had my share of rainy days! Be that as it may, there is a solution to any dismal day and that I should think would be spending time with you.

You've heard me say more than once, "Thanks for loving my daughter." I mean it. Thanks for loving her so much that you have changed who she is, too. It doesn't stop there, your daughters have been infected with the same positive outlook on life, drilling it down to a daily routine of laughter, anticipation, and hope. A man can bestow many gifts and attributes on his family, but none as important as character. Your own character will be challenged at times throughout your life, but when built on concrete, it will remain unmovable by the world and its continual attempt at altering who we are as men. Your greatest defense against the slew of insults, bad business dealings, angry mobs, and fearful people is to remain emphatically positive, which is really the same thing: emphatic and positive. More easily said, stay positively positive!

An enemy would think twice before firing upon the man who chooses to be positively positive because it's like a superpower that has shielded you. However, life does have a way of finding those crevices whereby, little by little, the harsh reality of life might slip in. If and when that happens, remember where your positive outlook comes from, for it is from your heavenly Father. Just as He touched Jeremiah's lips and encouraged him not to be afraid, I am confident God is with you and will protect you.

The world is changing, and the Lord will soon gather His own. Until that time, gird up thy loins and arise, and be positively positive in your love for Him. Furthermore, teach these things to your beautiful daughters so that they might know the truth of where your joy comes from. "Keep looking up" is more than just the secret of life, Charlie Brown, it is the joy of a soon-expected King! To know you, Dustin, is to greet each day positively positive!

Elya

I recall being afraid for you, very afraid, only once in my life…and now, choose not to reflect on that time, for it was a cold and terrible night and no longer has any bearing on my life or yours. However, I am confident that night and the many dark days that followed made you the person you are today, a champion of happiness.

The universe has conspired and chosen to make happiness a very real part of your existence. Everyone around you in every circle of life will experience your happiness. It is not to say you are always happy, or have something to be euphoric about. It is, however, something that has become a real part of you to the point that happiness is contagious when people are around you.

I don't need to tell you how much the world, needs happiness these days. Everyone is so far removed from it; the idea of being happy has become a distant fantasy that now seemingly requires a compass and a lengthy journey to recover.

You, Elya, I believe are that compass. We both believe that God and Jesus Christ are the source and the ultimate creators of happiness, but like the North magnetic pole, a compass is required to point us to the source. Therefore, I believe you are a good source to point people to the Father. Call it magnetism, call it happiness, you are the apex, a good place to find a healthy dose.

This happiness drives a secondary characteristic that is equally noteworthy; optimism. Optimism is just another way of saying happiness, but the world of today requires both in separate doses. A spoonful of happiness and you set the mood. A happy *good morning, hello, it's good to see you,* and the atmosphere is suddenly light, any possibility of aggression averted, and gentleness is invited in. A shot of optimism and the world is suddenly in agreement. Doubt vanishes, depression turns to hope, and sorrows to peace.

What must it be like to be in your presence and experience real happiness and optimism? I'll tell you.

For a mother of three little children whose husband was killed in a car crash this year, who doesn't know why God would do such a terrible thing, who can't find a way to let God into her heart…she found the compass that will lead her to the source eventually.

To three single women who have been friends since birth, more like favored aunts, you have been a continual source of encouragement and hope as you've opened up your family's life so they too could experience it.

Your happiness and determination gave a Hollywood "has been" cowboy the courage to overcome age and defeat and teach a young girl the skills of horsemanship and instruction. Ultimately, I believe you had a part in restoring his marriage and passion for life.

A divorced rancher gave you a job shoveling manure which you turned into a horse training career, and gave her the comfort and friendship she needed.

I'm not an optimistic person, Elya. Far from it, unfortunately. Yet, in your presence, I aspire to greater things and have a deep desire to find that within myself. That's how magnetic stuff works, you know. Rub a magnetic object on a nonmagnetic metal object and, suddenly, it has magnetic properties of its own. Thus, it too becomes a compass pointing to the ultimate source.

To know you, Elya, is to be attracted to the source. The ultimate source of happiness, joy, and optimism, Jesus Christ and His beloved Father. Bless you, for the light you shine for the lost and hopeless every day of your life.

Isabelle

I'm a big believer that life

changes as much as you want it to

Martin Freeman

The hankering to change the world will forever be at the core of your existence, Isabelle. Not because the world needs changing, not because you're unhappy in the world you're in, but because you see beyond its misty blue sphere and into the microcosm of which it is a part.

Your mother, was and is, much the same. At a young age, she possessed the ability to experience life in a way that brought an eagerness for today and anticipation for tomorrow. It wasn't impatience or regret for the things of today, it was a knowledge that had an objective with purpose. Bill Johnson, of Bethel Church, someone I greatly admire, once said, "You weren't made for yesterday or for the past. You were made for today; you were made for tomorrow." I think you know that, Isabelle, because it is how I see you experience life. You are fearless. Unafraid to voice an opinion, unafraid to take a challenge, unafraid to step out in your pink leather cowboy boots and blithely say, "Let's go make some joyful noise!"

The world needs some happy noise. If more people were to think and live optimistically, present in today, yet filled with anticipation for tomorrow, the sun would rise on a warmer earth each day, and find creation aglow with…well, life. Life, and I think courage too.

One fall, I watched as you let each of your cousins and sister, Melody, ride on the back of your horse, Punky. They were all in town for your grandma and my fortieth anniversary. One cool afternoon we drove to the stables where you kept your horse. Your mother, with your help, got Punky ready and brought him out to the gate. The cousins were all eager, but a little timid as they didn't have horses of their own. What I saw take place, was that once you were on the back of Punky and rode around the arena, all the other kids suddenly had courage and were excited to ride too. One after another, each cousin took turns; Oz, Winry, Nausicaa, Hansel, Adelaide, and your sister Melody too. Oh, the thrill of riding a horse! I remember when I was young, I had a friend with a horse, and every so often, we would go to his home, he would saddle the horse, and let me ride around his pasture. It was one of the most delightful and thrilling parts of my childhood. I can still smell the matted hay in the barn, the manure in the pasture, the cool afternoon air. It didn't take place very often; and I wasn't a very good rider, I was always a bit fearful of the monstrous beast beneath my legs. What I remember most, was my friend, who was much smaller than me, coaching me and saying, "It's easy. Just take your time, talk to the horse, and let him do what he knows how to do." Which of course, was trot around the arena. All I had to do was hold on and have fun. That's it, I think. It isn't that you must change the world as much as that you want to tell others, "Have fun, take your time, and hold on!" Like the spinning carousel at the park that you stand on while someone spins it faster and faster. You know letting go will land you face down in the sand, so you hold on as tightly as you can! Take that same carousel and lie down on it on a sunny summer afternoon, letting the warm steel warm your back as you look up into the sky and gently turn yourself with your feet buried in the sand. A completely different feeling, but one wherein you're in control. In control of the beauty that surrounds you, simply because you paused long enough to lie back and enjoy it. To know you, Isabelle, is to experience life at two extremes. One like the spinning carousel that can change at a moment's notice, bringing with it excitement and the thrill of wind in your hair. The other is like lying back on the warm carousel without motion; calming, letting life fill every part of you. In those two extremes, the world is changed. Most people live in the middle of those two extremes. Too afraid to accelerate, and too hurried to slow down. You, Isabelle, possess the courage to change the world, and in those moments, allow the rest of us to see life more clearly.

Now, consider again those words by Bill Johnson, "You weren't made for yesterday or the past. You were made for today; you were made for tomorrow." God created you to be able to encourage others to see the world more clearly. Because of your thrill for life, and joy in living every day, you help others see God more clearly too. So the next time you're lying on your back on a carousel in the warm sun, looking up into the warm blue heavens, take a moment and thank God that He made you who you are; optimistic and filled with joy.

Melody

"Trust?" The word that I imagine is going through your mind as we stare at one another from across the table. You're eating cherry cheesecake while sitting on your father's lap, and I'm sipping a glass of homemade Sangiovese. It's not the first time we've had this match, staring at one another's eyes for long periods trying to understand what the other is thinking. For the longest time, you wouldn't leave your mother's arms, not even for your father's. You were content to be held by her and content to not be touched; or, for that matter, spoken to by anyone you didn't trust. Ah, there it is again, that word trust. *All the world is made of faith, and trust, and pixie dust,* wrote J.M. Barrie for his character Peter Pan. I think he is right, and I think, Melody, you've got a little of each of those medicines inside of you. Trust has to be worked out to its purest form because it's not something you can just have a wee bit of. Trust is something that requires heaps and gobs and extra dribbles of speculation and attention. Trust comes after much observance, and is only credible when it blossoms in that someone you're trusting.

Faith is much the same as trust, but even harder, because faith requires that you move from a position of safekeeping and into a position of belief. That's harder, especially while you sit on your father's lap and eat cheesecake, and watch me sip my red wine. I don't have anything you want, and nothing nearly as good as cherry cheesecake!

When the last crumb of cake was eaten and you tired of supper, you made your way to the floor and quietly sauntered around behind your mother's chair. I pretended not to notice. A moment or two later, you slowly moved a little closer to where I sat. I continued my conversation with your mother; I think we were talking about Christmas traditions as I slowly pushed my chair away from the table. Turning my knees out from under the tablecloth, I held out my hands and turned to see if you trusted me enough to come into my lap. Without hesitation, you ran to me and let me scoop you up, place you on my knee, and give you a big squeeze. That's faith, Melody, the moment you took action and jumped into my lap. You moved from trust to faith. Assurance that I was okay and I meant you no harm. Oh, and what a pleasure it was to hold you so close and listen to you chatter about horses and Christmas trees, cowboy boots, and cookies. I looked into your eyes, and you mine and we giggled.

Holding you in my lap reminded me of how much God desires to hold us on His lap. He wants us to trust Him, then, with a leap of faith, jump into His arms and tell him about all the things that are important to us, like cowboy boots and cookies.

Having faith is making yourself free to fly in this world, Melody. The ability to soar above the world and experience the beauty and love God wants us to experience every day. If Peter Pan could fly without pixie dust, he'd have faith too. We don't need pixie dust, we just need God to help us trust others and step out in faith.

It was the week before Christmas, and your parents had to get you home to bed. We had a wonderful dinner, and the air outside was cool, but refreshing. You didn't need my hand to help you down the steps; you were very brave and strong and said, "I got it."

At the bottom of the stairs, you turned and looked at Grandma Terry and me and said, "I uv you guys." My heart melted.

There's something I didn't mention about that night. I was feeling a little sick and I was very tired and even a little discouraged. We can get like that sometimes when life seems too overwhelming and we find it hard to get through a day. I had lost a little bit of trust in people, and faith in God, and

I didn't have any pixie dust to pick me up and help me fly or feel happy. The words spoken on a cold crisp Christmas Eve; "I uv you guys," reminded me that, to know you, Melody, is to have faith. Faith in one another, faith in a God who loves us. Thank you. Grandma and I uv you too!

Punky

The fragrance always stays in the
hand that gives the rose.

Hada Bejar

Do you recall all the flowers we stole from the little ice cream diner in Durango? We never got caught, but we made off with dozens over the years, giggling as we rushed out the door into the cool night air. Never hand in hand or arm in arm because you hadn't allowed me in too close, but always heart to heart. We were penniless, working for Cross Bar X Youth Ranch but somehow we were always able to find enough coins in the seat cushions and ashtray of my VW Bug. Movies were too expensive, and so we bided our time meandering the old western streets, watching the steam plume skyward from the steam locomotive, or wandering through the cemetery overlooking the Animas River and the city below. We talked of so many things we wanted to do with our lives. What kind of houses we might like to live in, and what type of work we could do to survive without having to have real jobs. Where we wanted to live and where we wanted to adventure! The dreams were too many for one evening of reveling so we would go back to the ranch and sneak into the lodge where we could continue our conversation over bologna sandwiched between lettuce and white bread smeared with yellow mustard. Into the night we continued our conversation, our dreaming, our infatuation with what the future might hold.

Unbelievable, isn't it? The adventures, the dreams, the travels, the children, and the grandchildren that have filled our lives. It is fair to say it is staggering to look back on our lives and all that God has blessed us with. Yet even more staggering for me is the unwavering love you have poured into our marriage, friendships, and children. It was Mark Twain who said, "Kindness is a language which the deaf can hear and the blind can see." Your heart is filled with such incredible kindness for others, it has more than once been the grace that saved others from my ill temper or impudent wrath. I'm ashamed to admit it, but it's true. You are a glue of beauty that has bonded together hearts, relationships, and our marriage of forty-one years. You'll be the first to admit, I know, that Jesus is the center of your gluey heart, but that's an honest admittance. If anyone has let Jesus transform them, it is you.

I laugh when you tell me you are going to write a note to someone, or a thank you note for the kindness someone has shown you, because rarely is the note filled with rambling indebtedness, but instead it is filled with scripture. You're not ungrateful, and your lack of personal words is never missed because your cards are filled with Grace, Hope, Love, and the voice of Jesus. To know you, Punky, is to be glued to Jesus.

To Know Me

The man who esteems himself in any regard

is a man of folly and pride. The er-

ror of his way may easily be reformed

through the simple act of forgiveness and service to others

E W Helmick

Rick Lawrence once wrote, "*People who live out a secure identity, striving to help others, are conduits for transformation in the world.*" I've never had a secure identity, yet I thrive on serving others relentlessly in hopes of transforming the world. When it comes to calculating my life failures and successes, personal failures outnumber the successes with staggering odds. Yet when I consider those I have served, those whose lives I have tried to better, I find myself smiling with a degree of satisfaction. It's folly and pride to think I've changed the world to any degree by helping others, but the satisfaction I speak of is more the idea that, more often than not, I was able to turn attention away from self and focus it on someone deserving. Paul Farmer, the American medical anthropologist and physician, wrote, "If I am hungry, that is a material problem; if someone else is hungry, that is a spiritual problem." Thus, I find myself operating in a spiritual realm almost all of the time. Not a spiritual realm that qualifies me as holy or spiritual, or religious to any degree, but spiritual in the sense that that is where I find my identity, serving others. It is easy to notice when I'm there. I'm silent, pensive, tearful, lost inside my soul. It's like Oz's talking of the soul with itself. Or Nausicaa's kaleidoscope, Melody's faith, Isabelle's hankering for change, Hansel's smiling heart, Gil's agreeable identity, Winry's fervor, Mile's strength, Caleb's happiness, Adelaide's coin pinched between her finger and the wall, Abby's unconditional love, Kanna's trust, Tuck's compassion, Hunter's courage, Tasha's love spread as thick as an avocado, Tiana's tender love, and Elya's happiness. My identity comes from each of your strengths, and I find I am happiest and most content when I am operating in that spiritual place.

If I find my identity through my bloodline, can you imagine how God feels when he sees His children operating in a place of serving others rather than serving themselves? He must get a great deal of satisfaction from watching us walk like Christ, serving others, not waiting to be served. Putting others first is one of the easiest things to do when we're paying attention to the world around us and not the world inside of us. The world inside of us stems from too much television, too much social media, and too much comparison. The world around us is pleasant and palatable as long as you're willing to take the time to taste it. For me, it has taken decades to learn how to be content with my own life and not compare myself with others. Everyone has a story, and every story will be different. Some grand, some sad. Some people's lives are filled with joy, while others are filled with drama. The key is to be content with your life and the blessings God has bestowed upon you. To know me, is to be surrounded by my children, grandchildren, and beautiful bride as we embrace the short season of life on earth with the greater expectation of eternity together with God our Heavenly Father.

There is a key to God's blessings in life. Simply draw close to him, giving Him everything you have, and trusting Him with every moment, worry, fear, money, and anxious moment. Not long ago, while sitting alone quietly before the throne of God, I felt the urge to write a manifesto of things I believed, but more importantly, things that could help me in the years ahead. It is my hope they will be a source of encouragement and hope to each of my children and grandchildren. This book may have been published and there are still grandchildren yet to come. Perhaps I'll draft a second volume, but if I don't, and if for any reason, you, my grandchild were omitted, it was only because time is short and life even shorter. Be encouraged therefore, that should you give your life over to Jesus and trust Him with all your heart, we will meet one day in the clouds, and what a glorious day that will be. Be sure

to look me up when you arrive! I'll leave my number at the gate!

E W Helmick Manifesto

Don't let yourself sink low

Don't be caught off guard by bitterness

Don't hesitate to forgive others

Don't hesitate to forgive yourself

Don't daydream without one foot already in action

Turn your sulking into serving

Turn your criticism into building

Lift something heavier than you

Jump off something taller than you

Run circles around your fears

Laugh at the devil

Invite angels to your dining table,

children to your quiet place,

the Spirit to your side;

the sinful side and the faithful side

Wake up Holy, go to bed thankful

When you want something admire it from afar

When you need something buy it

Don't move to a new place or change careers unless God calls you

Don't wait for God to call you if your heart is complacent, He won't

If God isn't speaking, take action, step out in faith, move

Expect radical experiences with God through your faith

Make faith a bigger part of your life.

Jump higher, step farther, and listen louder.

Tell others about Christ and experience revival in your life

Get off your tail and do something daily for others in bold

service and thanksgiving to your King, God Almighty

* * *